IT'S TIME TO EAT CILANTRO

It's Time to Eat CILANTRO

Walter the Educator

Silent King Books
A WhichHead Entertainment Imprint

Copyright © 2024 by Walter the Educator

All rights reserved. No part of this book may be reproduced in any manner whatsoever without written per- mission except in the case of brief quotations embodied in critical articles and reviews.

First Printing, 2024

Disclaimer

This book is a literary work; the story is not about specific persons, locations, situations, and/or circumstances unless mentioned in a historical context. Any resemblance to real persons, locations, situations, and/or circumstances is coincidental. This book is for entertainment and informational purposes only. The author and publisher offer this information without warranties expressed or implied. No matter the grounds, neither the author nor the publisher will be accountable for any losses, injuries, or other damages caused by the reader's use of this book. The use of this book acknowledges an understanding and acceptance of this disclaimer.

It's Time to Eat CILANTRO is a collectible early learning book by Walter the Educator suitable for all ages belonging to Walter the Educator's Time to Eat Book Series. Collect more books at WaltertheEducator.com

USE THE EXTRA SPACE TO TAKE NOTES AND DOCUMENT YOUR MEMORIES

CILANTRO

It's time to eat, come gather near,

It's Time to Eat
Cilantro

Cilantro's fresh, let's give a cheer!

Green and leafy, so light and small,

It adds great flavor, we'll love it all!

Snip, snip, snip, the leaves we'll take,

For soups, or tacos, or rice to make.

It smells so bright, like a garden breeze,

Cilantro's magic puts us at ease.

Sprinkle it here, sprinkle it there,

On guacamole or what we prepare.

It dances on food, like a little crown,

Making each dish the best in town!

Try it on rice, or in a stew,

Cilantro's taste is fresh and new.

With every bite, the flavor pops,

A leafy joy that never stops.

It's Time to Eat
Cilantro

Some like it bold, some like it light,

But cilantro's taste is just so right.

A pinch on veggies, a pinch on meat,

Cilantro makes each meal complete.

Chop it finely, or leave it whole,

Add a handful, it's good for your soul!

Green and tasty, it shines so bright,

Cilantro's always a pure delight.

Mix it in salsa, stir it in dips,

It's Time to Eat
Cilantro

Taste the wonder on your lips.

It's fun to eat, and good for you,

Cilantro's flavor is fresh and true.

Now when it's time to enjoy your plate,

Cilantro's waiting, don't be late!

With every leaf, your smile will grow,

It's the tastiest green you'll ever know.

It's Time to Eat
Cilantro

It's time to eat, come gather near,

Cilantro's fresh, let's give a cheer!

Green and leafy, so light and small,

It adds great flavor, we'll love it all!

So grab a bunch and give it a try,

Cilantro's a treat you can't deny.

It's time to eat, so let's all say,

It's Time to Eat
Cilantro

Hooray for cilantro, it's a yummy day!

ABOUT THE CREATOR

Walter the Educator is one of the pseudonyms for Walter Anderson. Formally educated in Chemistry, Business, and Education, he is an educator, an author, a diverse entrepreneur, and he is the son of a disabled war veteran. "Walter the Educator" shares his time between educating and creating. He holds interests and owns several creative projects that entertain, enlighten, enhance, and educate, hoping to inspire and motivate you. Follow, find new works, and stay up to date with Walter the Educator™ at WaltertheEducator.com

Milton Keynes UK
Ingram Content Group UK Ltd.
UKHW010227111224
452348UK00011B/551